Balboa Press books may be ordered through booksellers or by contacting:

Balboa Press
A Division of Hay House
1663 Liberty Drive
Bloomington, IN 47403
www.balboapress.com
1 (877) 407-4847

ISBN: 978-1-9822-4832-1 (sc)
ISBN: 978-1-9822-4833-8 (e)

Library of Congress Control Number: 2020910137

Print information available on the last page.

Balboa Press rev. date: 11/10/2020

BALBOA.PRESS
A DIVISION OF HAY HOUSE

MOM
and
DAD,

I CHOOSE YOU!

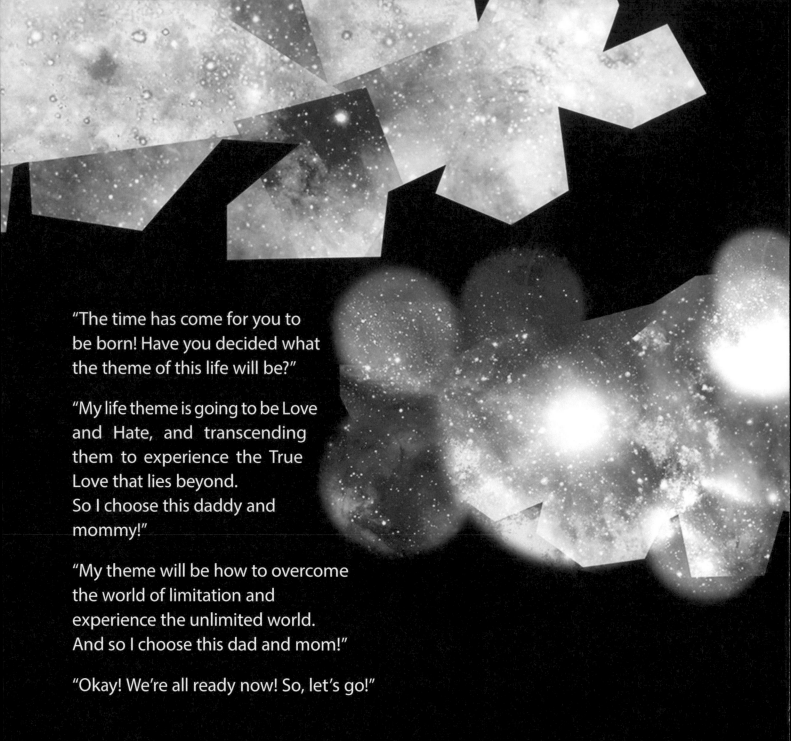

"The time has come for you to be born! Have you decided what the theme of this life will be?"

"My life theme is going to be Love and Hate, and transcending them to experience the True Love that lies beyond.
So I choose this daddy and mommy!"

"My theme will be how to overcome the world of limitation and experience the unlimited world.
And so I choose this dad and mom!"

"Okay! We're all ready now! So, let's go!"

MOM and DAD, I CHOOSE YOU!

Hidden Traps in the Parent-Child Relationship

ROSSCO

Maru is a little girl who loves picture books.

Every night before going to sleep, she looks forward to her mother reading her a picture book.

"Time to go to bed, Maru! Which book do you want tonight?"

"Read me this one, Mom!"

"Sure!"

This is Maru's favorite picture book, the adventure of a little bear.

Smiling, Maru gets into bed.

"Sweet Maru, thank you for being born to us, your mommy and daddy!"

Before beginning to read, Maru's mother always thanks Maru for being born to them.

Maru feels very happy and peaceful when her mom tells her this.

Her father smiles at them lovingly.

"I came into this world to be your child because I love you, Mommy and Daddy!"

"Really? Did you already know us before you were born?"

"Yes! I was watching you from the sky and I told my friends that I would be born to you, this mom and dad!"

"Your friends?"

"Yes, my friends in the sky! Everybody chooses their favorite mom and dad!"

"Oh, I see."

"Have my friends all come here yet, I wonder?"

"It would be nice for you to see them all again, wouldn't it?"

"Yes. We will surely meet each other again, because we made a promise!"

"Oh, please let me know if you meet them!"

"Okay, Mommy, I will!"

Maru's mother is a bit surprised by Maru's story, but she soon forgets about it.

"Well, let's start reading!

The tiny bear's adventure begins!"

With the sound of her mother's tender voice, Maru closes her eyes and enters deep inside the tale.

Every day, every night, Maru's mother reads her a picture book.

And each time she tells Maru, "Thank you for being born to us!"

Maru always feels happy and peaceful.

One night just before reading, her mother speaks to her.

"You are going to have a brother, sweet Maru!

There's a baby inside of your mommy's belly."

"A baby?"

Her mother puts Maru's little hand on her belly.

"Yes, a baby boy. He is still very tiny, but growing quickly in my belly.

When the cherry trees blossom, you are going to be his big sister!"

"His big sister…"

Her mother looks very happy.

Maru, however, feels strangely lonely.

She feels envious of her baby brother, still in her mother's belly,
where he gets to stay together with her always!

Her mother worries when she sees Maru's gloomy little face,
but she tries to change the anxious mood.

"Maru, our sweetheart, thank you for being born to us!
Now, let's read our book!"

Every night her mother tells her "Thank you for being born to us!"
but tonight it doesn't make Maru happy.

Even with her eyes closed, the world of the picture book doesn't reveal itself to her.

A sensation of loneliness and anxiety overcomes her, as if her mother were leaving her
far behind.

Still, her mother continues reading to her every day, every night.
And before she knows it, the happy, peaceful feeling returns to Maru.

The night when her baby brother is born, Maru goes to bed all by herself. Her mother stays at the hospital with the new baby.

Her father holds her and comforts her, but Maru still feels lonely without her mother by her side. She gets into bed, covers up from head to toe, and curls up like a kitten.

"Mommy...."

Thinking about her mother makes her feel even lonelier, and her tears fall harder and harder.

It is the beginning of cherry blossom season when Maru's little brother comes into her life.

So tiny and soft and adorable!

Maru falls in love with her little brother.

"Sweet Maru, welcome your baby brother.

His name is Taku," her mother says to her while she nurses the baby boy.

"My sweet Maru, what a wonderful sister you are!

Love him tenderly," her father says as he strokes Maru's cheek.

Maru suddenly feels very grown up. Realizing that she is now his big sister fills her with strength from inside.

From the day of Taku's arrival, Maru's favorite hour before bedtime is forgotten.

Even with her mother home from the hospital, the precious moment doesn't return.

How she wants her mother to read her picture books! Maru tries again and again to tell her mother, but she can't, because her mother is always with her brother!

Seeing her mother smile so happily into her brother's little face, Maru feels so lonely that no voice comes out.

"Mommy, please look at me too!"

Maru says over and over to herself.

One day, her mother asks, "Say, sweetheart, Maru!

Would you look after Taku while I make him some food?"

"Yeah, all right."

"Thank you, my sweetheart.

What a good sister you are!"

Happy and proud at her mother's praise, Maru determines to take good care of Taku.

She gazes at the tiny little baby in his crib.

Taku looks back at her, all smiles.

"Goo goo, ha ha, hee hee."

To Maru's ears, it sounds like Taku is saying, "Sister!"

He extends his tiny arms and hands toward her, so she tries to give him her favorite stuffed teddy bear.

"Gawwww!"

Suddenly, Taku begins to cry and throws the bear away.

Maru's mother rushes in and takes Taku in her arms, trying to calm him down.

"What happened?

Oh dear, it's okay…"

Maru is filled with sadness.

She just wanted to be sweet to her little brother, and she ended up making him cry. She feels so bad!

"Is Mommy mad at me?"

She looks into her mother's face, but her mother only has eyes for Taku.

Maru feels abandoned, all alone, isolated. And a small negative thought arises in her.

"Mommy only thinks about Taku!

Maybe she doesn't love me anymore!"

In the corner of the crib, her adored bear lies sadly.

Seeing this, Maru suddenly explodes with all the feelings she has been suppressing.

"Aaaarrghh!"

Maru bursts into tears.

Tears upon tears stream down her face.

"What's happened to you, sweetheart?

Taku's crying wasn't because of you."

But her mother's kind words cannot stop her tears.

Maru's mother embraces her, waiting for her to stop crying.

"Oh dear, Maru, is anything hurting you? What's the matter, Maru?

Is something wrong?

Tell me anything. Talk to Mommy!"

Crying for a while washes away all her loneliness and bad feelings and calms her a little bit. Finally, she says,

"Mommy, read me a book again!"

Instantly, her mother understands.

"Maru has been lonely and sad, without enough attention.

Oh, I'm so sorry. Mommy didn't understand what you were going through!"

Then she speaks very tenderly,

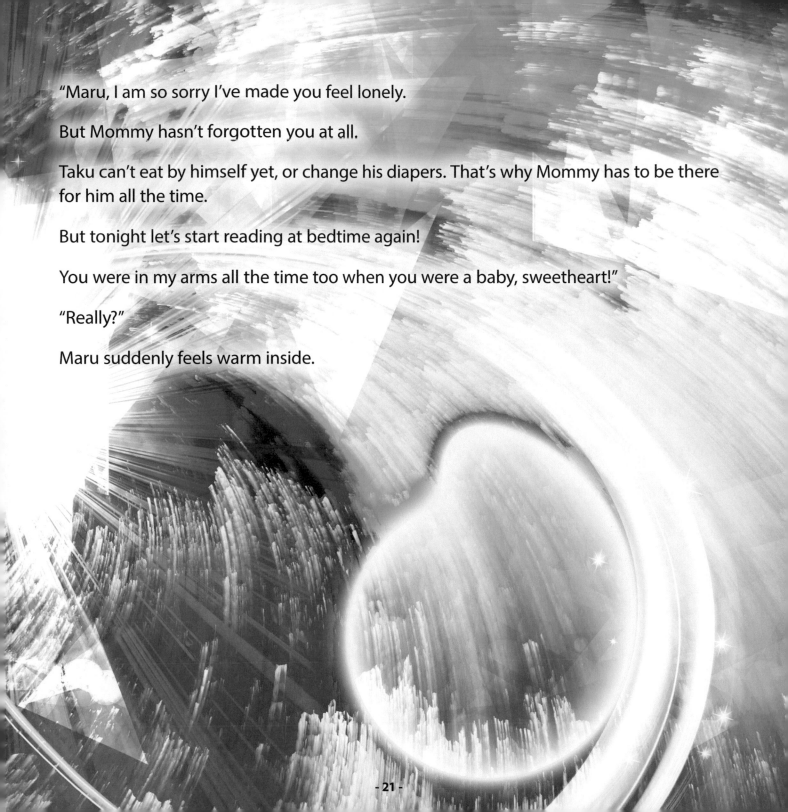

"Maru, I am so sorry I've made you feel lonely.

But Mommy hasn't forgotten you at all.

Taku can't eat by himself yet, or change his diapers. That's why Mommy has to be there for him all the time.

But tonight let's start reading at bedtime again!

You were in my arms all the time too when you were a baby, sweetheart!"

"Really?"

Maru suddenly feels warm inside.

Talking to Maru, her mother remembers when she was a little girl.

"When my little sister came, I also felt like she took my mother away from me.

Thinking that my mother loved my little sister more made me feel so sad and lonely that I became jealous of her.

But I can see how much I was loved by my mother then, just the way I love my daughter now."

Maru's mother gives her a big smile of thanks, finally understanding her own mother's love.

And she smiles again at the little girl she once was, whom she sees in her daughter, Maru.

That night.

"It's time to go to bed, sweet Maru! Which picture book would you like tonight?"

"I want this one!"

Maru brings her favorite book, about the little bear.

Happy and joyful, she gets into bed with a big smile and closes her eyes.

Her father and Taku are beside them too.

"Our sweet Maru and Taku, thank you for being born to us."

Maru is filled with happiness and peace.

She is sure that Taku feels the same way.

"Listen, Mommy.

Thank you too for being born to be mommy for me and Taku!"

Smiling, her mother opens the book.

"Okay, Maru, let's start little bear's adventure!"

The End

Hidden Traps in the Parent-Child Relationship

Explanatory Guidance

Introduction: Parenting is a process of love in which each parent returns to his or her own origin

Your life is the story you decided to live

What is a parent?

Our feelings toward our parents vary from person to person.

This book discusses parents and children, the relationship of origin within which humans are born. My hope is that you will fundamentally re-examine your life in order to fully enjoy each moment and find your greatest happiness in everyday life.

To begin, go back to the very beginning of your life and imagine your life as a movie.

Your film begins at the moment you come into the world.

Of course, you are the main character. You're also the author of the screenplay, the director of the movie, and you cast all the characters. You are the one who decides everything.

Your movie contains many life-changing turning points, decisions and hardships, growth and trials. As the story unfolds, you feel and taste a variety of emotions, your mind and heart mature, and you discover the true meaning of your coming to this world. You live your life in the brilliance of your own existence.

When you truly consider your life in this way, your idea of time and space and your view of life itself become completely different.

You create the film, so naturally you must know everything about the plot and the story.

Once you gain this perspective as the film's producer, you can watch calmly as it's projected on the screen, because no matter what happens, you know the entire story from beginning to end.

Unfortunately, the hero on the screen doesn't know what is going to happen.

How can it be that the main character, who should be the author and director of the film, doesn't know the story?

What if we think of it this way? What if before you were born, you were in the position of Observer, capable of producing the film, then at the instant of your birth, you became trapped inside the world on the screen.

You have completely become the hero and can no longer remember the position of Observer, because you believe, "This body is what I am." You inevitably perceive yourself based on the physical fact of having your own body.

In other words, at the moment of your birth you become imprisoned inside of the flat images and can no longer see the film you made as a film.

However, this can even be part of the scenario you wrote.

Perhaps knowing the story before seeing the film will seem boring to you.

Perhaps you erased these memories at the moment of your birth, because you wanted to have the "real experience" of being human.

Having lost your memory, you want to enjoy the process of regaining it through experiencing human pain and pleasure.

We could even suppose that with such ardent intention you have jumped into the screen.

In this way, we live without regaining our memory.

We even forget how to regain our memory.

So we may say our life develops unconsciously and proceeds as if tossed about by any number of different incidents.

Haven't you questioned the meaning of life and asked yourself, "Why did I come into the world?"

If you hadn't lost your memory about who you really are, those questions would never have arisen.

Unconsciously, you know, "This physical being is not my true self." That's why inside of you there is a desire arising to know who you really are, which won't be satisfied until you become what you are meant to be.

Ironically, this desire to know the true self drives us to seek it in the outside world—to live believing that the false self, or ego, which is created by others outside of us, is the real self.

Each of us has a physical body with which to experience the life that we determined before we were born. All the information you need to live your life is in your hands from the beginning. Yet you are unable to use this information if you continue to live life as a false self, in other words, ego.

You may be unable to live well, and feel restricted, experience trouble, and face problems throughout life, and just think that's the way it is.

Then, when your life ends you will leave your body again.

The film ends, you come out from the screen, and return to the position of Observer. But you no longer have your body with which to experience life.

If we believe that our human lives occur in cycles over and over again, we seem to keep repeating, "By a lucky chance I was born, and I made the same mistake again! But, next life for sure...!"

We compared a human life to a movie—now, what would happen if we could gain the eyes of the producer viewing the entire story as we live it? We would see so much nonsense caused by our being stuck inside the screen.

I call this the world's "trap," and what I'm going to describe is the system to unlock this trap.

This system is the art of regaining the memory that we have lost.

You've been unaware of this trap, but once you see it for what it is you can escape from the world in which you've been stuck.

From that instant, both you yourself and your life will change completely, as if you'd been reborn.

We come into this world having already determined our own life.

This time, for certain, the process of becoming your true self can begin.

This may be impossible to believe through conventional thinking, but I know you will understand for the first time what it's all about when, knowing the system, you can gain a complete view of your own life from the position of producer.

We come into life choosing our father and mother, in order to live the life theme we alone have determined

Your life story starts when your mother and father first meet, because without this encounter you never would have come into being.

Until now you've probably taken for granted that you were born because your father and mother got together. But what if instead you came with full intention, casting your mother and father yourself and setting up their encounter? Wouldn't this cause a radical shift in your feelings toward your parents and for the children who have chosen you for their parent?

And if, in fact, you know that all your ancestors were chosen by you in order for you to be born as what you are now, your cosmic view or view of life itself would change completely.

With a different father or mother or just one single ancestor missing, you would not be here now as what you are.

The probability of your parents' encounter, which produced "what you are," is astronomically small. Even more astonishing, the binding of the single sperm and egg that was the origin of "what you are" is nothing short of a miracle.

In such a transcendental "life system," which is beyond human wisdom, there is a hidden secret we have never imagined.

Within you flows the same blood you inherited from your parents.

Biologically, you have a total of 46 chromosomes, 23 from your father and 23 from your mother, that enabled "what you are" to be born and exist.

What this means is that in your paternal and maternal genes you have been given all the proper and suitable information you need to pursue the life theme you decided before your birth. It's as if you said, "I want to live according to this theme, and want to experience real life by overcoming it. That's why I choose to be born to this mother and father!"

Your life, which chose your parents and jumped into the human dimension according to the genetic information given by your father and mother, repeats its cell division inside your mother's womb and creates "what you are."

If before your birth you chose to manifest as a particular sex, for example by saying, "I want to try being a man" or "I want to experience life as a woman"... the simple act of living now as a man or a woman would demonstrate to you the mystery of life.[*]

We normally take being alive for granted and live without questioning why we were born or why we exist here and now. But in fact we are born with perfect timing as a result of an incredible number of miraculous events happening one after the other.

A totally new life occurs through the fusion of man (one terminal pole) and woman (another terminal pole), which are akin to positive (plus) and negative (minus), death and life, good and bad, disease and health, past and future, and so on. When these extremes of opposite energy fuse, they energetically produce something totally new. I call this phenomenon "marriage."

---

[*] To clarify, the Miross system welcomes and benefits all individuals, and does not exclude or discriminate against people of any sexual orientation. Miross is about a person's inner male and female and the energetics between them. Whether you are heterosexual, homosexual, transgender, or bisexual, you are made of two opposite polarities—that is, two sexes called maleness and femaleness that exist in you. This is because everyone is born from a father and a mother and inherits 23 chromosomes from each one. The union of these two energies, specifically maleness and femaleness, is the essence of Miross. You are to discover your true Self through your partner whether he or she is male or female.

Your being what you are is a result of this "marriage" between two extremes of polar energy. Just as your father (man) and your mother (woman) fused in perfect balance, so are you born as a perfect being.

This perfect being was born with a story that is already complete. There is no other life more secure and perfect than this.

Every being exists as a unique and powerful individual destined to be born only once both in the past and the future.

In order to enable anyone to manifest and live in the individuality of their original nature, I would like to clarify one by one the "traps" in which humans are stuck, and to explain to you the art of regaining your lost memory of origin.

Trap I: People see their entire life through their innate ego

Life's greatest trap is hidden in the parent-child relationship

It is commonly believed that childhood is the most important period for the basic formation of personality, and that this is determined by how parents relate to their child. This is why lately more and more parents seem overly nervous about their children's education.

In fact, children are frequently hurt very deeply through their education and behaviors that seem normal or inconsequential to parents.

You too may have been traumatized by a casual remark or deed of your father or mother.

But do the ways parents treat their children really have such great influence on a child's personality and life?

For example, why do brothers or sisters with the same parents, who were raised with the same amount of affection, have different impressions of their parents?

A mother would say she loves her children equally, but one child may feel that he wasn't loved while another grows up certain of his mother's tender care.

The trap is hidden here in the huge difference that siblings raised under the same circumstances see in their mother.

Children see their parents as indicators of their own value

For children, parents are the origin of life, and therefore unquestionable absolute beings.

As they learn the basis of human relationships from these absolute beings, children experience a variety of emotions for the first time.

When accepted by their parents they experience a sense of security and trust, and when rejected they experience insecurity and mistrust.

When praised by their parents they experience the joy of acceptance and the sense of peace that comes from feeling loved, and when scolded they experience guilt, despair, and the terrible sense that they are unworthy—feelings that may give rise to hatred and anger.

However, the way you view your parents' treatment of you is based on your own feelings. In fact, you may never know what they were actually thinking.

Being accepted or rejected, loved or not loved—these are not things your parents gave you, but rather feelings based on how you perceived their treatment of you.

Furthermore, the reason you viewed their treatments this way is that when you felt you were "accepted" or "loved" by them, you were at the same time accepting and giving recognition to yourself.

On the other hand, when you felt you were "not accepted," you were at the same time rejecting yourself.

Siblings growing up under the same circumstances can hold different impressions about their parents because they see themselves from different viewpoints, meaning their self-esteem differs completely from one another.

If the way we view our parents' treatment depends on how we esteem ourselves, when does our sense of self-esteem begin?

In general, it is believed that children begin to judge themselves according to their parents' valuation of them, for example when they are praised or scolded.

But if our self-esteem creates the way we view our parents, that very self-esteem is actually the driving force, and the way we view our parents only a consequence.

When children feel something toward their parent for the first time, they already possess a particular sense of self and view their parent through this perspective.

In fact, we already possess our sense of self when we are born. That self-esteem can be said to be your innate ego, which you need in order to live and manifest the life theme that you decided before your birth.

We are stuck in an astonishing trap, in that what we feel about our parents is meant to be how we think of ourselves, or in other words, our self-worth.

It's commonly thought that a newborn baby does not yet possess an ego—that not until 6 to 18 months of age does he begin to realize that his body is his self and recognize that all people except him are others. That's why it's believed that ego development occurs during that period.

However, recognizing that "you are your body and your body is you" allows your innate ego to arise and enables you to embody your life theme through your father and mother.

This knowledge has shaken the foundation of conventional child-rearing and education, as our preconceptions about the self being created by the behaviors and words of our parents become no longer applicable.

For example, in Maru's story she becomes jealous of her new baby brother for taking up her mother's time and thinks, "My mommy doesn't love me."

If you have a brother or a sister, you may have had an experience like Maru's at some point.

Children expect their parents' absolute affection, constantly asking them, "Watch me, look at me, love only me." Children are extremely sensitive about whether or not they are loved.

If they don't receive their parents' affection as often as they want, children may feel that they are not loved.

To the mother, both children are adorable. She is just busy taking care of the younger one, who is more in need of her attention.

"My mother doesn't love me" is a false belief on Maru's part. Usually, we are not even aware of these preconceptions.

Even if Maru does become aware that her belief is false, the sense of lacking it creates inside of her will not be erased.

That's because her feeling that her mother doesn't love her actually stems from her own belief that she is not worthy of love.

The feeling of being unworthy of love will remain with her forever unless this preconception is removed.

Otherwise, she will continue to pick up on cues that she is unloved based on her mother's behaviors, reinforcing her own ego's false belief.

Parents may never dream that their beloved children see themselves this way, even at such a young age.

But, as mentioned previously, the "innate ego," which is necessary for the life theme that the child has decided to be born with, starts to emerge around the time he recognizes everyone except him are others.

Each of us has a life theme that centers on what we need to overcome and clear.

We might call the theme Maru has chosen "love and hate."

Your belief about yourself, based on your innate ego, creates everything you see

What will happen if Maru, who believes that she is not loved by her mother, continues holding onto this belief?

There are many cases of people whose lives become miserable because their younger siblings are born.

Unfortunately, in most cases people are not even aware of the unexpected cause.

Some time ago, when I was counseling a lady whose outrageous jealousy caused her to struggle in partnerships and other relationships, something totally unexpected, even to her, came to the surface.

At first glance, she seemed to be an independent woman far removed from jealousy and conflict, and eager to improve her situation and realize her dreams.

Surely something must have triggered her behavior.

The first trigger occurred in childhood, when she came home from school sobbing because a friend blocked her way as a joke.

Her mother responded, "Don't keep crying about it. Why don't you tell them to stop!"

She wanted to be helped and supported, but her mother didn't provide that.

She wanted comforting words, but her mother didn't offer any.

Feeling betrayed, she thought, "My mother will never help me."

She felt abandoned by her mother.

According to the trap, how you view your parents' reactions is how you evaluate yourself. The woman who felt neglected by her mother considered herself unworthy of maternal love at the same time.

After that, she stopped expecting anything from her mother, no longer depended on anyone, and refused to cry in front of others.

Believing that her mother would never help her, she determined to live independently and become as strong as possible on her own.

For her mother, "Why don't you tell them to stop!" was simply a fair and correct thing to say, but for the daughter it was a shocking event.

Digging deeper, her jealousy was rooted in her younger brother's arrival.

Until then, her mother's affection had been showered on her alone, but suddenly it seemed to be directed entirely toward the new baby. This was hugely stressful for her.

Having decided to be independent, however, she went on playing the role of the nice and caring sister.

In doing so, she must have been overwhelmed by bitter feelings such as her hidden jealousy toward her brother, the sadness of being unable to depend upon her mother, and hatred for not being cared for.

Convinced that she was abandoned by her mother, she would take away from her mother's words and actions only those elements that supported the idea that she was unloved.

In intensifying the innate ego that told her she was unworthy of love, she was only hurting herself.

That is why she began exhibiting strange behaviors around the time of her brother's birth.

She began to suffer from a mild eating disorder, got into mischief that was beyond what one would expect of a small child, and developed unexplained fevers.

All of these actions and conditions were symptoms of her frustration in not being able to ask for her mother's attention.

Gradually she suppressed the bitter emotions and unfulfilled desires in her heart in order to stop feeling them.

As she grew older, whenever something happened that reminded her of her childhood, the old wound ached and the suppressed emotions erupted in the form of jealousy.

Thus even a blessed event like the birth of a brother can become the axis from which someone's life spins out of control, depending on how they view their parents in early childhood.

It's likely that most people have felt at times that they were unloved in their parent-child relationship.

"Love" is an eternal theme for all mankind, and anyone who holds to that theme simultaneously suffers from its opposite, "hatred."

Here is another example.

A woman who struggled for 15 years with conflicts with her father was stunned when she discovered the true cause of her hatred for him.

In early childhood she was involved in a serious accident that almost killed her. Later, she was told by her mother that her father, who worked abroad, did not bother to come back and see her.

"Your father never came back for you. What a cold heart!" Hearing this became a trigger for her to believe her father didn't care for her at all.

Since then, her father's every behavior seemed to prove to her that he did not love her.

In her eyes, her father was just someone who praised her big sister while judging her own value solely on her achievements in school, or dashed her hopes by making icy comments like "What's the use of that?" when she showed an interest in anything.

When she became an adult, she was convinced that her father was the cause of her unhappiness, and she hated him.

Finally she woke up when she discovered the trap: that her belief about her father was identical to her belief about herself, a fiction created by her innate ego.

She realized that her belief that her father didn't care about her and that she wasn't loved was based solely on the fact that she saw herself as someone unworthy of love.

She began to understand that this low valuation of herself and her feelings of worthlessness were what had been holding her back her entire life.

When she escaped from the trap, the clouds that had obscured her vision disappeared and the world returned to her in full color and brightness.

Freed from the illusion caused by her misunderstanding about her father, her painful memories of the past were transformed into warm, happy memories.

"My father has always loved me....."

When she finally recognized his paternal affection, she felt a sensation of energy flowing from the bottom of her being, as if blood had started to move through her body for the first time.

More importantly, her father, who knew nothing about her transformation, became a completely different person.

Her cold-hearted father suddenly became the caring father she had never known, and their parent-child relationship changed into a trusting one, as if they had been close from the beginning.

By understanding the trap and overcoming false beliefs that you could never have seen clearly on your own, the world around you changes all at once in just this way.

How you value your parents' judgment, how you view their acts and behaviors—these are all your own beliefs about yourself.

In other words, what you see is not your parents' intentions, but rather the judgment you make toward yourself.

You believe in a "self" that doesn't exist, made from layers of preconception generated by your innate ego, and view the outside world through these layers.

Trap II: Childhood wounds determine your romantic relationships

We view romantic partners through the same lens with which we viewed our parents based on the world of false assumptions

For a daughter, her father is the first person she encounters of a different sex, and her mother the first person of the same sex.

Likewise for a son, his mother is the first person of a different sex, and his father the first person of the same sex.

The way people view romantic partners is based on the way they viewed their own father and mother.

A woman chooses a partner based on her feelings about her father, while a man chooses based on his feelings about his mother.

But no matter how you view your parents, they are seen through your own filter, which is solely your belief.

This belief was created by your innate ego in order for you to experience the life theme that you determined for yourself.

As you grow up, your view of your parents is turned toward potential partners. In this way, you are not viewing that person, but rather yourself.

It may be hard to imagine, but what you are seeing when you look at your partner are your own beliefs about yourself reflected in them.

For example, if you believed as a child that you were unloved, it actually means that you lacked confidence in being loved and despised yourself for that.

Because you believe that you are not loved, you make a conscious effort to be loved in your relationship.

You constantly worry about how your partner sees you or thinks of you. This concern occupies your mind, and as a result your attention is only on yourself.

The truth is that you are not really seeing or hearing your partner, only yourself.

Seeing only yourself is the cause of misery and failure in romantic relationships

If you only pay attention to yourself, constantly worrying whether you are worthy of your partner's love and trying to secure their love, you end up pretending to be someone you're not in order to be loved.

You may spend your time scanning your partner's face for signs, or give up the things you like to do, or even give up seeing your parents because your partner doesn't feel comfortable being with them. The longer you pretend, the more you are living as a false version of yourself.

Unless you escape from the world of false beliefs that you created through your relationship with your parents, you will continue to experience the same phenomena that you did with them.

Take for example a wife who becomes resentful of her husband's judgmental assumptions about her, and feels wronged and ignored. This is actually the world she has created from her own perspective, based on false beliefs.

When she was young, her father tried to define her by saying, "You are this" or "You are that," and she felt her existence was totally negated.

This had nothing to do with what her father was actually thinking; rather, it was what she believed to be true.

She was merely projecting her judgment of herself as a bad and unworthy child onto her father.

Many people carry the wounds of feeling unloved during childhood.

From the moment we feel unloved, we focus all of our attention on doing what we think we need to do in order to be loved.

Our belief that we're unloved brings forth the reality of being unloved.

Even if we meet the partner of our dreams, or change our partner to fit our ideal, we cannot be happy.

Then we either try harder to be loved, or we give up on being loved.

Whichever we choose, if we continue to negate ourselves, our romantic relationships will fail.

Furthermore, we tend to attract other phenomena that negate ourselves in areas outside of our romantic relationships, such as our health, finances, and relationships with others.

Nothing will change if we hold onto the false impression of ourselves that was created through our relationship with our parents and continue to see the world around us through this lens.

On your own, you can't see these false beliefs clearly.

Only through your relationship with your partner can you discover the hidden key that will release you from the world of illusion and lead you to your real self.

Trap III: Whatever a parent suppresses in childhood appears in their child

Another trap is hidden in a parent's view of their child

Difficulties in parenting occur when we are unable to understand why our children act the way they do.

They are our own children, yet we have no idea where their characteristics and behaviors come from.

And since we tend to see children's incomprehensible behaviors as problems, we try to correct them and steer them in the direction we think is right.

But no matter how much we scold them or nag at them, there is no chance that they will change.

As a result, many parents worry about their children's future, anxiously wondering how to guide them.

As the trap tells us, the way we judge others is actually the way we judge ourselves. If, then, a parent's view of their child is really their own nature reflected on the child as on a screen, what do the child's inexplicable behaviors say about the parent?

Deep in our hearts, we carry the things that we had to bear as children in order to survive, keeping these bitter feelings so suppressed and hidden that even we cannot recognize them. These very things are now appearing in our children.

We don't remember that we have suppressed these feelings, but we unconsciously display the very personality traits that are the opposite of what we have hidden inside.

Because parents don't see these issues as their own, they try desperately to correct their child, whom they can't understand.

Here are some examples of how the issues that parents have suppressed in themselves appear in their children.

- A fun-loving child who was not allowed to play becomes a parent whose own child fools around and refuses to study.

- A child who grew up in an environment of sexual repression becomes a parent whose child is promiscuous.

- A child whose parents did not allow him to have his way becomes the parent of a child who is willful and stubborn.

What this means is that children do not behave the way their parents want them to.

This sometimes causes parents to become frantic, not knowing how to handle their children, and may even lead to abuse.

But no matter how hard parents try to improve their child's behavior, nothing will change until they understand that the very issues they suppressed in their own childhood are showing up in their children.

So how can parents understand their "suppressed self" through their child? Here's an example of the trap.

A child comes into life carrying what the parent lacks or has lost

"My child speaks her mind. She's so different from me.

It's good that she has a strong will, but it gets to be too much. She just insists she's right and doesn't listen!"

One mother who came to me for a consultation was worried because only scolding could make her daughter be quiet and listen.

The total opposite of her daughter, she was the type of person who hides her own opinions and feelings rather than expressing them.

As she told me about her childhood, I saw that the things she had suppressed back then were appearing in her daughter.

As a child, she was often scolded by her mother and told to speak her mind clearly.

In actuality, she was not unclear at all. She had distinct ideas and opinions, but she found it hard to express them well.

Her mother often told her, "I never know what you're thinking! I don't understand you!"

Parents are an absolute presence in their child's life.

Therefore, their words remain in their child's memory for a long time, and the child believes what they say.

If a parent scolds a child for being sneaky or impatient, that's what the child grows to think about himself.

The woman I counseled believed that she was hard to understand because that's what she was told by her mother.

This, then, is the situation that she chose to be her life theme.

Unknowingly, she accepted her parents' insensitive words and created her own wounds in her heart, believing that she was what she had been labeled.

Scolded and told too often by her mother to speak clearly, she became afraid to speak up and believed that she was stupid and bad for being unable to express what she felt and thought. She then felt guilty for feeling that way.

Yet inside herself, her thinking was clear. That is why her belief that "no one understands me" grew stronger and stronger and she began to express herself less and less.

Suppressing her thoughts and feelings, and becoming resentful toward her inappreciative mother, she rarely argued back at all.

In short, she suppressed her own clarity.

This suppression was now coming out in her child, who was direct and frank in speaking her mind.

Your child expresses what you suppressed as a child

Just understanding that what you are seeing or feeling in your child is what you suppressed in childhood makes parenting easier.

Additionally, your child will be able to grow up with his heart and spirit intact, because he is no longer judged for what he expresses.

The mother I counseled was liberated from the bitter emotions she had felt as a child, by acknowledging through her daughter what she herself had suppressed in childhood. As a result, her feelings toward both her mother and her child were totally changed.

Her daughter in turn began listening to her mother rather than insisting on her own way.

When children are small we worry less about their behavior, but as they grow, the situation becomes more serious and may lead to social withdrawal, truancy, bullying, and other forms of delinquency.

Most parents do everything they can to seek help, including counseling from specialists, but too often they find no solution.

By contrast, we have many examples of parents reporting that their children's various issues were resolved once they, the parents, discarded their longstanding beliefs and discovered through their own child what they themselves had suppressed in childhood.

The things you have suppressed are not necessarily "bad."

To the extent that you suppressed your feelings as a child, your children will, on your behalf, do the things you wanted to do but gave up on because of the circumstances you faced.

In the case of the mother I counseled, her daughter was perhaps using herself to send the mother a message along the lines of, "Mom, don't be afraid. It's okay for you to speak your mind!"

Young children in particular may express their personality very explicitly, which parents sometimes find troubling.

But when we realize that our children are expressing what we ourselves were unable to express in childhood, they become even more precious to us.

When your children discover something they like or want to do, it's important to respect their wishes without expectations and allow them to pursue and nourish their dreams.

Creating a proper environment for them to flourish will free your own suppressed wishes inside of you, helping your children blossom and grow their abilities in ways you never imagined.

Children's ideas and behaviors show us that every one of us is unique.

For parents, there is no greater reward.

Indeed, your children are a message and a gift.

By understanding the system, you can overcome anything

I have tried to demystify the traps hidden in the parent-child relationship, realizing that you may never have considered the idea that our own beliefs and assumptions could completely derail our lives.

What's more, these beliefs were not given to us by our parents, but created through our own self-regard.

If you think you are "not loved" by your parent, in fact you are seeing in them the projection of your belief that you are unworthy of being loved.

I call these our "parent-seeing eyes," and through them we see everyone and everything around us.

While it may seem as though you see other people and things as they really are, you are actually projecting onto them constantly from the limited world of your mind, based on your beliefs.

The true nature of this belief is your life theme: "What I want to overcome as a human being."

Experiencing the theme requires your "innate ego": the ego you were born with.

The belief born from your innate ego produces self-denial and a sense of guilt in you, and from there countless inner conflicts like jealousy and attachment emerge, derailing your life.

In short, we live a life built upon false belief and assumptions.

The self that you believe is "you" is in fact a fake self created by your innate ego.

Through this fake self, you have considered many things, made choices, resolved issues, and lived the best life you could, but you have been living without stepping a foot outside of the world of the thinking mind created from your false beliefs.

Living this way, you can experience the life theme you have chosen, but you will be stuck inside of the theme and never able to overcome it. You will spend your whole life never living your true story.

Because the suffering we experience in the form of conflicts and disappointments as adults may originate within the parent-child relationships of our childhood, we may turn to psychotherapy, which attempts to solve problems by determining their root cause in past events.

While this can provide temporary relief, people often find themselves relapsing into their same problems.

If we merely determine our conflicts and false beliefs without understanding the cause, our problems will never end.

All the problems we experience in modern life, including relationship issues, physical and mental illness, job and money worries, and problems with our children, can be understood within the origin of the person involved—that is, within the parent-child relationship in which the personality was formed.

Once you discover that you are stuck inside of this trap and understand what it is and how it came to be, the rest is simple.

What you need to do is to escape the limited world of your mind and demystify everything you falsely believed was true, from the position where you have an entire overview of your life.

This position, from which you see existence in totality, is the position of the "Observer," which was discussed previously in the book.

This vision of totality is the "parent-child system," and by viewing your entire life within this system, the illusory tragedy that you have lived over and over will come to an end.

You will understand that the father and mother you have been seeing do not exist anywhere, but are an illusion created by your beliefs, and that you are and indeed have always been loved.

When you recognize this trap and understand the system of the parent-child relationship, your wounds and trauma of the past will be completely healed—even the wounds of the parent-child relationship that your ancestors have lived and passed on repeatedly throughout ancestry.

These wounds and difficulties will no longer be passed to your children and future descendants, and you will be able to live in a world of absolute peace that no human has yet experienced.

So many difficulties and hardships happen throughout life.

Whatever seemingly impossible problem you face is merely a phenomenon that exists within the life you have designed. By seeing this phenomenon as it actually is and confronting it with courage, you can absolutely overcome it.

We ourselves created the story of our life, determined the issue we need to overcome, and chose the most suitable father and mother to enable us to manifest our life theme.

We have such extraordinary powers of creation that we actually give birth to ourselves into the world.

When returned to the position of the Observer, this creative force can be fully manifested.

I invite you to discover the traps inside your own parent-child relationships, to transcend the life theme you have determined, so that you can design for the first time a new life story that brings you true happiness and joy, and live it to the fullest. This is what I now and forever ardently wish for you, with all my heart.

Afterword

This book, with its focus on the parent-child relationship's tremendous influence on the formulation of the personality, is based on the principles of New Dimensional Thought Technology: Miross.

It features a combination of two parts: first, a picture book featuring a commonly occurring situation between parent and child, and second, a guide to the traps inherent in the parent-child relationship.

We come into the world having already created our story of life, having determined the life theme we need to overcome, and having selected the most appropriate father and mother who will enable us to manifest that theme. This groundbreaking insight offers readers an opportunity to reconsider their own life.

Many of us have been hurt deeply in childhood by our own parents' words and actions, and many of us hold onto hatred toward our parents. Through the Miross system each of us can now use these feelings for our father or mother to discover our "inner consciousness," and understand how this consciousness is built upon illusory thinking, feelings, and emotions passed on from generation to generation.

As you have learned, your real-life father and mother are merely illusionary images of the father and mother that you yourself created by projecting onto them the thought patterns engraved within your genes.

Until you discover the true identity of these feelings, you will be unable to break the negative chain that has been repeated throughout generations of ancestors.

This is why destiny is said to be inherited.

When you come to understand the traps in relationships and transcend the life theme that you have determined, your life will return to the past to be reset. Finally, it will be your turn to live and manifest the real purpose of your life—to discover why you are here.

People who have mastered this system report that they now understand and forgive their parents through their relationship with their own children. At the same time, the child they once were is healed, along with their present self. The memory of their past is entirely rewritten into a new life, filled with love.

One mother who was obsessed with education came to understand that she was projecting the inferiority she felt from lacking higher education onto her son. Once she realized she was trying to cover up her own sense of inferiority, both mother and son were freed from endless hours of study and entered into a new life where they could live and enjoy hobbies as they liked.

In the end, her son's grades didn't suffer. Instead, he developed his potential and gained admission to a highly selective college.

Another person reported that his decades-long feud with his father resolved instantly, and they were able to regain a trusting relationship as if the discord had never occurred.

This happened when he realized that the father he had been seeing was merely an illusion of his father created by his thought pattern.

There are many more examples of people whose parent-child relationships were dramatically changed and whose lives were completely transformed by learning the Miross system. To find out more, visit our website at http://rossco.jp/.

Since its publication, this book has been read in many ways. It has launched a movement of storytelling and reading that has spread from kindergartens and elementary schools to nursing homes all over Japan. I hope it will continue to be read widely by more people from many different fields, positions, and circumstances, because its subject matter—the relationship of parent and child—is the most basic and universal of all.

By learning the traps in the parent-child relationship, anyone and everyone can transform themselves, and each and every family can reinstate its bond—creating a wave of change throughout society. This is my conviction and my wish for you all.

Printed in the United States
By Bookmasters